The Nativity

The True Story
Of Christmas

MARK WEIMER

LIFE CONNEXIONS
PEACHTREE CITY, GA

The Nativity — The True Story of Christmas

Published by Life ConneXions
The Publishing Group of Campus Crusade for Christ
375 Highway 74 South, Suite A
Peachtree City, GA 30269
To order: (800) 827-2788

All Scripture quotations, unless otherwise indicated, are
taken from the Holy Bible: New International Version,
© 1973, 1978, 1984 by the International Bible Society.
Published by Zondervan Bible Publishers, Grand Rapids,
Michigan.

Printed in the United States of America

ISBN-10: 1-56399-280-9
ISBN-13: 978-1-563-99280-3

Table Of Contents

Introduction

Today, Christmas is celebrated in many parts of the world. We see bright lights; we give presents; we sing songs.

But what is the real meaning of Christmas? Christmas is the celebration of a remarkable birth — the birth of Jesus Christ, who came to earth as the Son of God over 2,000 years ago.

So, together, let's take a look back in time — to the very special time when Christ was born. Let's take a journey to the first Christmas.

In The Beginning

"In the beginning was the Word, and the Word was with God, and the Word was God. He was with God in the beginning.

"Through Him all things were made; without Him nothing was made that has been made. In Him was life, and that life was the light of men. The light shines in the darkness, but the darkness has not understood it.

"There came a man who was sent from God; his name was John. He came as a witness to testify concerning that light, so that through him all men might believe. He himself was not the light; he came only as a witness to the light. The true light that gives light to every man was coming into the world.

"He was in the world, and though the world was made through Him, the world did not recognize Him. He came to that which was His own, but His own did not receive Him. Yet to all who received Him, to those who believed in His name, He gave the right to become children of God…

"The Word became flesh and made His dwelling among us. We have seen His glory, the glory of the One and Only, who came from the Father, full of grace and truth...No one has ever seen God, but God the One and Only, who is at the Father's side, has made Him known."[1]

Christmas is the story of how the Word of God — who is God — became a human being and came to live among us.

CHAPTER 1

The Story Begins

Elizabeth lived a little over 2,000 years ago by the city of Jerusalem in Israel. Jerusalem was already at this time a very old city — over 1,500 years old. It was the home of the Jewish people, and at the center of Jerusalem was the temple — the place where they worshiped God.

Elizabeth lived with her husband Zechariah, who served as a priest in the temple. This godly couple had one great sorrow — they had no children, because Elizabeth was unable to have children, and they were both well along in years.

For any couple wanting children, the inability to conceive can be heartbreaking. However, at this time in Israel, it was doubly heartbreaking, because children — particularly sons — were the way in which the family line was carried on.

One day, it came to pass that Zechariah, in his priestly duties, was chosen to go into the temple to burn incense. This was a great honor, and while he was inside all the assembled worshipers were praying outside.

Suddenly, an angel of the Lord appeared before Zechariah. "When Zechariah saw him, he was startled and was gripped with fear. But the angel said to him: 'Do not be afraid, Zechariah; your prayer has been heard. Your wife Elizabeth will bear you a son, and you are to give him the name John. He will be a joy and delight to you, and many will rejoice because of his birth, for he will be great in the sight of the Lord. He is never to take wine or other fermented drink, and he will be filled with the Holy Spirit even from birth. Many of the people of Israel will he bring back to the Lord their God. And he will go on before the Lord, in the spirit and power of Elijah, to turn the hearts of the fathers to their children and the disobedient to the wisdom of the righteous — to make ready a people prepared for the Lord.'

"Zechariah asked the angel, 'How can I be sure of this? I am an old man and my wife is well along in years.'"[1]

Even when an angel appeared to him, Zechariah did not believe — he wanted to know how he could be sure. Before we are too hasty in judging Zechariah, how would you and I respond? Would we respond in faith — or respond in doubt?

"The angel answered, 'I am Gabriel. I stand in the presence of God, and I have been sent to speak to you and to tell you this good news. And now you will be silent and not able to speak until the day this happens, because you did not believe my words, which will come true at their proper time.'

"Meanwhile, the people were waiting for Zechariah and wondering why he stayed so long in the temple. When he came out, he could not speak to them. They realized he had seen a vision in the temple, for he kept making signs to them but remained unable to speak.

"When his time of service was completed, he returned home. After this his wife Elizabeth became pregnant and for five months remained in seclusion. 'The Lord has done this for me,' she said. 'In these days He has shown His favor and taken away my disgrace among the people.'"[2]

Just imagine Elizabeth's joy. Not being able to have children in those days was a disgrace, and God had finally removed her disgrace. He had accomplished it miraculously by allowing her to become pregnant when she was quite old. And now she was to have the joy of a son — and not just any son, but a son who would go on to prepare the way before the coming of the Lord. His name? History would know him as John the Baptist.

CHAPTER 2

Mary

When Elizabeth was in her sixth month of pregnancy, the angel Gabriel appeared again — this time in the city of Nazareth. While Jerusalem was a major, bustling city, Nazareth was a small commercial town in Israel located about 100 miles journey north of Jerusalem. While Jerusalem was large and prosperous, Nazareth was small and poor. While Jerusalem was a sophisticated city, with the leading intellectuals and merchants in Israel of that day, Nazareth had a reputation as a "rough and ready" town. A few years later, someone was heard to remark, "Nazareth! Can anything good come from there?"[1]

You may think that sightings of angels were common in those days, but they were not. In the entire Old Testament, spanning 1500 years of history of the Jewish people, sightings of angels were very rarely recorded. That's what makes what happened next even more remarkable. For an angel to appear to a priest in the temple of

Jerusalem, the center of religious life for all of Israel, was amazing, but for the angel Gabriel to appear in the rough little town of Nazareth — to a young teenaged girl — was unheard of.

Mary was the name of the young teenaged girl to whom the angel Gabriel appeared. How old was Mary? We don't know for sure, but we know that she was already engaged to be married. At that time in Israel, a common custom was for girls to be married in their early teens; husbands might often be a few years older. If we had to guess, we might suppose that Mary was about 16, and Joseph, her intended husband, may have been in his early 20's. In ancient Israel, the engagement period typically lasted one year. While a couple was not actually married during this engagement period, there was a legal contract to be married that could only be broken by divorce. We also know that Mary was a virgin — she had never had sexual relations with Joseph or with any man. She was saving herself until the time of her marriage.

Joseph was a carpenter — a humble but honorable profession. His family was neither wealthy nor powerful. However, he and Mary shared one particular distinction: they both were distant descendants of King David.

King David was the historic King of Israel who had ruled Israel one thousand years before the time of Mary and Joseph. It was David who defeated Goliath and expanded the kingdom of Israel. It was David who is revered as Israel's greatest king. In addition, the promised Messiah — the One who would save and redeem Israel — was to come from one of the descendants of David.

Other than the fact that Joseph was descended from David, there was nothing outwardly remarkable that we know about Mary and Joseph. Joseph was a carpenter, and we know that neither he nor Mary had a great deal of money. They lived in the town of Nazareth, several days' journey away from the main capital city. There was nothing outwardly to distinguish this young couple — but God had a magnificent plan for them.

CHAPTER 3

The Angel Appears

When Elizabeth was in her sixth month of being pregnant, God sent the angel Gabriel to appear to Mary. The angel said, "Greetings, you who are highly favored! The Lord is with you."[1]

Just think of the impact of this greeting on young teenaged Mary. She is not a princess, she is not a prophetess or a queen. And yet, not only does the angel appear to her, but in his greeting Gabriel says that she is "highly favored" and that the Lord is with her!

"Mary was greatly troubled at his words and wondered what kind of greeting this might be."[2] Wouldn't her reaction of being "greatly troubled" be a natural one — the same as you or I would have? First, Mary has an angel appear to her; and then, she is told by the angel that she is highly favored and that God, the God of the universe, is with her.

In ancient Israel, God occasionally appeared to holy men and women. Yet He was still God —

the one true God, who created heaven and earth. He was powerful and just, He was merciful, and He was loving; but He was also a God to be held in great reverence. When one ancient prophet had a vision of God, he felt he would perish because he had actually looked upon the almighty and all powerful God.

So for Mary to be told "The Lord is with you"[3] was an incredible thing, but it was only the beginning.

The angel Gabriel went on to say, "Do not be afraid, Mary, you have found favor with God."[4] So the angel knew or could sense her fear, and he wanted to encourage her. What does it mean to find favor with God? To find favor with a ruler of that day meant for the ruler to choose you as someone special to receive his blessing.

CHAPTER 4

The Promise Of Jesus

The angel continued to Mary, "You will be with child and give birth to a son, and you are to give Him the name Jesus. He will be great and will be called the Son of the Most High. The Lord God will give Him the throne of His father David, and He will reign over the house of Jacob forever; His kingdom will never end."[1]

The name Jesus is not just any name; it means "God is salvation." So the angel is saying to Mary that her son, Jesus, is salvation. We will talk more about salvation later, but, in short, it means to be saved — in the case of mankind, to be saved from our sins. So Jesus, the Son of God, is the One who is our salvation.

Here, to this young teenaged girl Mary, comes an incredible proclamation. The angel says that Mary will become pregnant and give birth to a son, and that Mary is to give this son the name of Jesus. Think of the tremendous impact that Jesus has had upon the world in the 2,000 years since this time!

What can we tell about this child, Jesus, from what the angel has said so far? The child will be born miraculously, to a virgin (remember, Mary is not yet married and has had no sexual relations). The child's name will be Jesus. Jesus will be great; and not just great in human terms, but He will be called the Son of the Most High — the Son of God. So Jesus will not just be a great man, He will be called the Son of God.

Gabriel also says that God will give Jesus the throne of His father, David. We know that Mary was a descendant of David, and that since Mary was His mother, Jesus would be both the Son of God and also a descendant of King David. But Jesus would not just reign on His throne for a few years as an earthly king; He would reign over Israel forever and His Kingdom would never end.

Jesus would be an eternal King, born of a virgin and called the Son of God. Can you imagine what Mary's response might be?

CHAPTER 5

Mary Responds

Who could blame Mary if she was overwhelmed at the angel's statements? She had been told she would have a child while she was still a virgin; that the child would be called the Son of God; that His name would be Jesus, meaning "God is Salvation;" that God was with her; that she was highly favored; and that Jesus would reign as King forever and ever in the kingdom of His father David. This was the promise that for hundreds of years the Jewish people had waited for — their Savior, their Messiah.

So how did Mary respond? She asked the angel, "How will this be since I am a virgin?"[1]

This is amazing. When Zechariah was promised by an angel that his wife would bear a son, his response was skeptical and even doubtful — "How can I be sure of this?"[2] While this may be understandable — you or I might quite possibly have responded the same way — it was basically Zechariah's way of saying "Give me another sign,

I am not sure about this." As a result, Zechariah was stricken dumb and was unable to speak for the next nine months.

Mary's response, however, was very different. She did not challenge the angel. She did not ask for another sign. She did not appear unsure, or ask "How can I be sure of this?"

Just picture how you would have responded if you were Mary. Here you are, a teenaged girl engaged to a carpenter. You are told you are miraculously to have a son who is the Son of God. What if no one believes you? What if people reject you? Why should you be picked out of all the women in the world for this incredible privilege?

Instead, Mary just asked how it would come to pass since she was a virgin. Her response was one of humble faith and confidence, simply asking how God would bring this miracle about.

CHAPTER 6

The Virgin Birth

When Mary asked the angel "How will this be since I am a virgin," the angel Gabriel answered, "The Holy Spirit will come upon you, and the power of the Most High will overshadow you. So the Holy One to be born will be called the Son of God." [1]

The angel makes it explicitly clear that no man will have relations with Mary, and yet she will give birth to Jesus. The child Jesus will be the son of Mary and will also be called the Son of God.

Further, the angel says that Jesus, who is yet unborn, will be the Holy One. To be holy means to be perfect, to be set apart for God, and never to sin. Holiness is a term which is usually reserved for God alone, because unfortunately all people on this earth sin. Jesus will be the Son of God, and He will also be the Holy One, the One who never has sinned.

The angel then encouraged Mary, "Even Elizabeth your relative is going to have a child in her old age, and she who was said to be barren is in her sixth month. For nothing is impossible with God."[2]

Elizabeth and Mary were relatives. They were possibly cousins, or perhaps Elizabeth, who was older, was an aunt or great aunt. What we do know is that Mary and Elizabeth knew each other, and that they lived a hundred miles' journey apart. For Mary to learn that Elizabeth, who was known to be barren and elderly, was also to have a child must have been a great encouragement.

The important thing to remember is what the angel said: "Nothing is impossible with God."[3]

CHAPTER 7

The Faith Of Mary

Mary has just been told of even more incredible things. How is she to respond now? Mary now understands that she will truly stay a virgin and yet give birth to a child. The way this will happen is that the Holy Spirit of God will come upon her.

In all of recorded history, a virgin had never given birth to a child. This was long before the days of artificial insemination and modern science. Such a birth simply could not happen without a miracle. Even more amazing is that her child would forever be called the Son of God. As further encouragement to Mary, even her relative Elizabeth, who was old and barren, was now going to have a child.

Who among us might not respond with skepticism, with disbelief or with doubt? Yet Mary's response was this: "I am the Lord's servant…may it be to me as you have said."[1] Mary responded in faith. She did not doubt; instead, she submitted herself to God and His will.

Truly God had chosen well the woman that would be the mother of His Son Jesus. She was not chosen because of her wealth, power, position, or fame. Instead, Mary had a heart of faith that obeyed God without doubt or skepticism.

CHAPTER 8

Mary Visits Elizabeth

As soon as the angel left her, "Mary got ready and hurried to a town in the hill country of Judea, where she entered Zechariah's home and greeted Elizabeth."[1] Mary showed her faith by believing the angel and leaving right away to see Elizabeth. Mary traveled several days to Elizabeth's home, in the hills in Judea near Jerusalem.

"When Elizabeth heard Mary's greeting, the baby leaped in her womb, and Elizabeth was filled with the Holy Spirit."[2] This baby, who was in Elizabeth's womb, would grow up to be John the Baptist. He leaped in Elizabeth's womb at hearing the voice of Mary, the mother of Jesus.

In later years, the lives of John the Baptist and Jesus would be intertwined. John the Baptist would be the prophet who would go before Jesus and proclaim to Israel that the Lord was coming. Jesus was the Messiah, the Prince of Peace, the Savior of mankind. John the Baptist would baptize Jesus and declare Him to be "the Lamb of God, who takes away the sin of the world."[3] Jesus would tell His followers that "among those born of women there has not risen anyone greater than John the Baptist."[4] Jesus would die crucified on a cross to pay for the sins of the world. John would also meet an untimely end, killed by the evil King Herod.

Yet at this point, both were babies in their mothers' wombs; and John, the baby in Elizabeth's womb, leaped for joy when he heard the voice of Mary, the mother of Jesus. Elizabeth herself was filled with the Holy Spirit of God.

Then in a loud voice Elizabeth exclaimed to Mary, "Blessed are you among women, and blessed is the child you will bear! But why am I so favored, that the mother of my Lord should come to me?"[5]

Elizabeth proclaimed Mary blessed among women. Truly Mary was blessed, as she was chosen by God among all the women on earth to bear His Son, Jesus. Elizabeth also proclaimed that blessed was the child, Jesus, that Mary would bear.

How did Elizabeth know that Mary was pregnant? How did she know that Mary had been blessed by God and that the child would be blessed? There were, of course, no emails or telephones. Mary had come to see Elizabeth as soon as the angel had appeared to Mary, and Mary had not yet even told Elizabeth what had happened. However, because Elizabeth was filled with the Holy Spirit, God had supernaturally communicated to her that Mary was pregnant.

Elizabeth also acknowledged that the child Mary was bearing was Elizabeth's Lord. Jesus was no ordinary child; He was not even just an especially godly child. Even though He was still in Mary's womb, Jesus was already Elizabeth's Lord.

Elizabeth concluded, "As soon as the sound of your greeting reached my ears, the baby in my womb leaped for joy. Blessed is she who has believed that what the Lord has said to her will be accomplished!"[6] Elizabeth proclaimed that not only was Mary blessed because God's favor was on her, and not only was Mary blessed because she would bear the child who was the Son of God, but Mary was blessed because she believed that what God had said to her would be so. Mary was blessed for her faith.

CHAPTER 9

Faith

Why is faith so important in our story? Already, we begin to see a pattern emerge — some people respond to God in faith while others do not.

Zechariah responded in skepticism to the angel. He said "How can I be sure of this?"[1] Even though an angel appeared to him, he still wasn't really sure. As a result, the angel Gabriel said, "Now you will be silent and not able to speak until the day this happens, because you did not believe my words, which will come true at their proper time."[2]

Contrast this with Zechariah's wife Elizabeth at the time she met Mary. Elizabeth knew and proclaimed by faith that the mother of her Lord had come to her, even when she had not been told. She proclaimed Mary was blessed among women, even though Mary was just a young teen-aged girl. And think of Mary's response, when given the amazing news that even as a virgin she would give birth to the Son of God. The penalty for being an unwed mother in ancient Israel could be death by stoning, and she would be subject to humiliation. Even though she believed God, who would believe her?

And what about her fiancé Joseph? How would he respond? Would he believe God's word or would he turn away from Mary? She had lived as an honorable woman, but now she would be unwed and pregnant. What did God have in store for her? In spite of all these concerns, Mary responded in faith.

What about you and me? We can say it was easy for Mary and Elizabeth, but was it really? They had not yet seen Jesus, and Elizabeth called Jesus her Lord before Mary had even told her she was pregnant. Mary submitted to God in the face of possible humiliation or even death.

So the same question exists for us today — how would we receive Jesus Christ? Would we receive Him in faith as our Savior and Lord? Or, like Zechariah, will we say with doubt "How can I be sure of this?"[3]

Just as in days of old, today we need to welcome Jesus Christ into our hearts and lives by faith as our Savior and Lord. Our response in faith is the key.

CHAPTER 10

The Magnificat

Mary's response to Elizabeth's greeting has been called the Magnificat. This is because the opening word of Mary's response in Latin is "magnificat," which means to glorify.

Mary responded to Elizabeth, "My soul glorifies the Lord and my spirit rejoices in God my Savior, for He has been mindful of the humble state of His servant. From now on all generations will call me blessed, for the Mighty One has done great things for me — Holy is His name."[1]

Even though she had just recently heard such amazing news, Mary's immediate response was to glorify God. Her spirit rejoiced in God, and she called God her savior. Interestingly enough, the phrase she used, "God my Savior," means almost the same thing as her son Jesus' name — God is Salvation. She acknowledged God as her salvation, and also proclaimed that God cares for her and that God watches over her even in her humble state.

Even as a young girl, Mary knew that God had done great things for her. She proclaimed that future generations would call her blessed, which has indeed been the case. Mary continued, "His mercy extends to those who fear Him, from generation to generation. He has performed mighty deeds with His arm; He has scattered those who are proud in their inmost thoughts. He has brought down rulers from their thrones but has lifted up the humble. He has filled the hungry with good things but has sent the rich away empty. He has helped His servant Israel, remembering to be merciful to Abraham and his descendants forever, even as He said to our fathers."[2]

These are impressive words of faith, spoken by a young girl. She proclaims God's faithfulness and His mercy, even in the midst of a country that is occupied by a foreign army, the Romans. Mary is truly a woman of faith.

CHAPTER 11

Mary Stays With Elizabeth

For the next three months, Mary stayed at the home of Elizabeth and Zechariah. This must have been an amazing time. It would have been Mary's first trimester of pregnancy — the first three months. How Mary and Elizabeth must have talked together about the amazing prophecies that were made to them. The same angel had appeared to both of them, and given to both of them a message prophesying the coming of the Savior.

Elizabeth was in her last trimester — the final three months before her baby was due. Picture the emotions of the two women! Maybe Mary and Elizabeth reinforced and encouraged each other. Most likely, they prayed together for one another and their soon-to-be-born babies, and reminded each other of God's faithfulness.

All the while, in the home was Zechariah, Elizabeth's husband. He was still unable to speak, and must have had plenty of time to ponder God's faithfulness and his own previous lack of belief.

For Mary, it could have been a time that challenged her faith. It is quite probable that at this time Joseph, her fiancé, did not know that she was pregnant. Mary was probably wondering what Joseph's response would be.

It was a time for Mary, Elizabeth, and Zechariah to wait, to think about John the Baptist, who would go before Jesus, and to think about Jesus, the coming Messiah. At the end of these three months, Mary returned home to Nazareth.

CHAPTER 12

John The Baptist Is Born

When the time came, Elizabeth gave birth to a son. Her neighbors and relatives rejoiced with her that "The Lord had shown her great mercy."[1] For Zechariah and Elizabeth to have a son miraculously in their old age was a great joy for all of the family.

Interestingly enough, Zechariah at this time was still unable to speak. Eight days later, the time came for the newborn baby to be circumcised, a Jewish ritual for all male children. This was also the time that newborn boys were given their names.

Those in attendance were about to name the baby Zechariah, after his father, which was the custom of the day, but his mother spoke up and said "'No! He is to be called John.' They said to her, 'There is no one among your relatives who has that name.' Then they made signs to his father, to find out what he would like to name the child. He asked for a writing tablet, and to everyone's astonishment he wrote, 'His name is

John.' Immediately his mouth was opened and his tongue was loosed, and he began to speak, praising God."[2]

Zechariah, during his nine months of not being able to speak, must have thought about the message of the angel, who had said that his son's name was to be John. Even though Zechariah did not respond in faith the first time he heard the angel, he did respond in faith now, and God blessed him.

Zechariah and Elizabeth's neighbors also heard about all that had happened. "The neighbors were all filled with awe, and throughout the hill country of Judea people were talking about all these things. Everyone who heard this wondered about it, asking, 'What then is this child going to be?' For the Lord's hand was with him."[3]

CHAPTER 13

Zechariah's Prophecy

Now let's look at what happens with Zechariah. Although he had responded with skepticism at the news that Elizabeth would bear a child, it is clear that he is now responding in faith. Zechariah was filled with the Holy Spirit, as Elizabeth had been when she greeted Mary. This was very unusual — in the times before Christ's birth, it was very rare for people to actually be filled with the Holy Spirit of God.

Filled with the Holy Spirit, Zechariah prophesied, "Praise be to the Lord, the God of Israel, because He has come and has redeemed His people. He has raised up a horn of salvation for us in the house of His servant David (as He said through His holy prophets of long ago), salvation from our enemies and from the hand of all who hate us."[1]

Zechariah recognizes the upcoming birth of Jesus, saying that God has raised up salvation through someone who is to be a child and descendant of David.

Zechariah was also speaking in faith, because he speaks of God bringing salvation to His people even though Jesus has not yet been born and nothing apparent has changed.

Zechariah went on to say that God will "show mercy to our fathers and to remember His holy covenant, the oath He swore to our father Abraham; to rescue us from the hand of our enemies, and to enable us to serve Him without fear in holiness and righteousness before Him all our days."[2]

He then spoke to his newborn son John, saying "And you, my child, will be called a prophet of the Most High; for you will go on before the Lord to prepare the way for Him, to give His people the knowledge of salvation through the forgiveness of their sins…"[3] Zechariah prophesied accurately that John would prepare the way for Jesus' coming. He would tell people about the knowledge of salvation, which is forgiveness of sins.

Zechariah then prophesied about the coming of Jesus: "The tender mercy of our God, by which the rising sun will come to us from heaven to shine on those living in darkness and in the shadow of death, to guide our feet into the path of peace."[4] Zechariah has truly become a man of faith.

CHAPTER 14

Joseph Finds Out

Meanwhile, Mary had returned home to Nazareth, just about the time that John was about to be born. She was now three months pregnant, and her pregnancy would soon begin to show.

Joseph discovered that Mary was pregnant. We don't know exactly how Joseph found out, although Mary may have told him herself. Joseph probably found out shortly after Mary came back from visiting Elizabeth, because soon after that it would have become apparent to people in town that Mary was pregnant.

Picture this situation! Joseph's beloved fiancée, Mary, was pregnant. Joseph knew that he had not had relations with her, so this could only have meant one thing to him — she must have slept with someone else.

For both of them, this would have been a disgrace and humiliation. For Mary, it could have meant even worse — the penalty for her having had relations with someone outside of marriage could be death.

Think of the destroyed trust between Joseph and Mary. He loved Mary and was prepared to marry her. She had gone away for three months to visit a relative, and now this? Imagine if this had been your wife-to-be.

Try to also picture Mary's emotions. She had received in faith the prophecy given to her by an angel — and now this? Think of how hard it would have been for Mary to remain full of faith at a time when her future husband was ready to turn her away. How would you and I have felt during this time?

Joseph must have been torn by a variety of emotions. It now looked to him as if his beloved wife-to-be had been unfaithful, and that he had been betrayed.

Joseph could now, if he wished, turn on Mary and subject her to the full scorn and judgment of the community. One option, if he chose it, would be to expose her and let her suffer the consequences. He would be humiliated, but his fiancée Mary would be disgraced and exposed to judgment.

Joseph was a righteous man, and he chose not to take this option. It is evident that he still loved Mary, even though he must have felt he had been betrayed.

Joseph decided to divorce Mary quietly. At that time in Israel, an engagement could only be ended with an actual divorce. If Joseph divorced her quietly, then Mary could perhaps move away to another village, and not suffer the public shame of what it had appeared she had done.

CHAPTER 15

Joseph's Dream

After Joseph had considered the option of divorce, an angel of the Lord appeared to him in a dream. It is interesting that God waited until Joseph had made an honorable decision about Mary before the angel appeared to him. Was God perhaps testing Joseph's character, to give him the chance to act honorably toward Mary even in the midst of such heartbreaking news? This might have been the case. Sometimes in our own lives, we may wish that God would tell us everything in advance, rather than allowing our faith to be tested.

Whatever the case, before Joseph actually divorced Mary, an angel appeared to him in a dream. Why a dream? God can work in many ways; while an angel had appeared directly to Mary and Elizabeth, the angel appeared to Joseph in a dream.

The angel said to him, "Joseph son of David, do not be afraid to take Mary home as your wife."[1] It is interesting that the angel addresses Joseph with the term of respect, "Son of David." To be called son of David, the greatest Jewish king, was a sign of great honor.

The angel does not begin by putting Joseph down, or criticizing Joseph for a lack of faith. He begins by showing Joseph love and respect.

The angel said to Joseph in the dream, "Joseph son of David, do not be afraid to take Mary home as your wife, because what is conceived in her is from the Holy Spirit.

"She will give birth to a son, and you are to give Him the name Jesus, because He will save His people from their sins."[2]

Joseph now has received the answer he was looking for — and what an amazing answer it is. The wonderful news is that his wife-to-be had never been unfaithful to him. Equally amazing is that Mary's child had been conceived by the Holy Spirit. The angel reassured Joseph that Mary is an honorable woman.

Now to Joseph comes an amazing revelation — that his fiancée Mary will not only bear a son but that the baby will be the Son of God. Joseph is to give this son the name Jesus, just as was told to Mary. He is also told that this Jesus will save His people from their sins. What an amazing revelation!

CHAPTER 16

The Name Of Jesus

What is in a name? To us today, names may have little meaning, and we often pick babies' names just because they sound nice. But in the time of Jesus, names often carried great significance.

Why was the baby to be named Jesus? As we have seen, the word Jesus means "God is Salvation." Usually, a baby would be given the name of someone in the family. For example, if Joseph was the father, the baby could be named after Joseph or one of his relatives. The name Jesus is important, because it is Jesus who will save His people from their sins — "God is Salvation." Jesus still does this today — He saves people from their sins.

We all need salvation — to be saved from present, past, and future consequences of our sins. Every time you think of the name of Jesus, you can remember — God is salvation. It is God who will save us through Jesus. It is a reminder that Jesus is God. His very name says God is salvation, and God Himself sent an angel to tell Joseph that Jesus would save people from their sins.

The normal human tendency, for ourselves as well as the people in Jesus' time, is to try to save ourselves. God says we can't save ourselves; only God can save us in Jesus. This is the central message of Christianity: Jesus is God and He saves people from their sins.

What is our response to be? It is to be a response of faith. Will we choose to receive Jesus as the Son of God who saves us from our sins? So far we have seen how Mary and Elizabeth received in faith the knowledge that Jesus, who was the Son of God, would bring salvation from our sins. We have seen how Zechariah first responded to the angel's prophecy about John in skepticism. We may not always get a second chance, but Zechariah did and he finally responded in faith.

CHAPTER 17

Isaiah's Prophecy

Hundreds of years earlier, a prophet named Isaiah had lived in Israel. A prophet in those days was someone through whom God both spoke and gave visions of what would happen in the future. Isaiah spoke many prophecies of the future. Some of his prophecies were of the Messiah, the Savior of the world, who was to come. Hundreds of years before Christ's birth, Isaiah had predicted that "The virgin will be with child and will give birth to a son, and they will call him Immanuel"— which means, "God with us."[1]

Isaiah also prophesied, "For to us a child is born, to us a Son is given, and the government will be on His shoulders. And He will be called Wonderful Counselor, Mighty God, Everlasting Father, Prince of Peace."[2]

Here now, in fulfillment of Isaiah's prophecy, the virgin Mary would give birth to a son. Even as the Apostle John said in his gospel, "In the beginning was the Word, and the Word was with

God, and the Word was God….the Word became flesh and made His dwelling among us."[3] In like manner, Isaiah's prophecy was that the son of the virgin would be "God with us," and truly, Jesus Christ was and is "God with us." The fulfillment of the prophecy had come as the virgin Mary gave birth to a son, Jesus, who is God with us here on earth.

CHAPTER 18

Who Is Jesus?

Think of all that we know already at this point in our story about Jesus — and He had not even been born yet!

Details about His coming had been predicted for centuries.

Jesus would be born of a virgin, the virgin Mary.

Jesus would be called the Son of God.

Jesus would also be known as the son of David. He would be born to Mary, who was a descendant of King David. He would reign as King forever, on the throne of David — not in an earthly kingdom, but an eternal kingdom.

Jesus would save His people from their sins. His very name says that God is salvation — and God sends salvation in Jesus.

God sent the angel Gabriel to Mary to tell her about the birth of Jesus. God sent the angel to Zechariah to predict the amazing birth of John the Baptist and his ministry, as well as the coming of the Savior. God sent an angel to Joseph, to tell him that the child born to Mary was the Son of God.

We also know the amazing news — that the Savior of the world would be born to a relatively poor, obscure young woman. Joseph was a carpenter living in Nazareth, an outlying town. Joseph was not a king, a ruler, or a wealthy business man.

We also know that our key response is to be one of faith. We know how Zechariah was judged for his lack of faith, and Mary was blessed for her faith.

Now, how would Joseph respond to the message he received from the Lord's angel?

CHAPTER 19

Joseph Responds

"When Joseph woke up, he did what the angel of the Lord had commanded him."[1] Joseph responded in faith and obedience.

It is interesting that it appears that Joseph's obedience was instantaneous. He did not question, he did not come back to God and ask for another vision. He didn't ask God, "How can I know this for sure;" he just obeyed in faith. Now Joseph knew the secret: there would be a virgin birth, and Jesus would be the Savior who would save the world from their sins.

After hearing from the angel, Joseph took Mary home with him to be his wife, but he had no relations with her until she gave birth to a son. Joseph was an honorable man and he knew the birth was to be a virgin birth; he also wanted to protect Mary from disgrace.

In the eyes of the town people, the birth of Jesus could then be legitimate, since Joseph and Mary would be married. Mary was protected from disgrace, yet was still a virgin when she gave birth to Jesus.

Joseph had joined the list of those who responded in faith to hearing the good news about Jesus.

CHAPTER 20

The Roman Census

Several months later, Mary was well along in her pregnancy. At that time Emperor Caesar Augustus, who ruled the entire Roman Empire, decreed that a census would be taken throughout the Empire.

Today, it may be difficult for us to understand the immense power of a Roman emperor. The Roman Empire stretched across Europe and through the Middle East into Africa. However, the fact is that today, 2,000 years later, the influence of Caesar Augustus is largely forgotten. On the other hand, the influence of Jesus, born to a humble teenaged girl in a far away province of the empire, has covered the globe. Earthly kings and rulers may have great influence for a time, but God's purposes will be accomplished.

The impact of taking such a census was huge, because everyone was required to travel to the town or city of their ancestral home. This meant that Joseph and Mary, who were descended from King David, needed to travel to Bethlehem, which had been the home of King David. Even though Mary was extremely pregnant and about to give birth, there was no exception. It was prophesied that the Savior, the Messiah, would be born in Bethlehem, and so, acting in response to the Roman census, Joseph and Mary prepared to go to Bethlehem.

While Nazareth was more of a rough commercial town, far from the center of civilization in Israel, Bethlehem was a small town just south of the capital city of Jerusalem. Although it was a small town, Bethlehem was a town of tremendous historical significance, because 1,000 years before it had been the home of David, Israel's greatest king.

CHAPTER 21

The Trip To Bethlehem

Joseph and Mary, acting in obedience to the Roman census, began the long journey to Bethlehem. Nazareth is in northern Israel, about 70 miles as the crow flies from Bethlehem. The actual journey, however, would have been more than 100 miles over the rough paths and roads of the day. It would have required going either through or around the city of Jerusalem. Additionally, there were hills and mountains, and the town of Bethlehem is 1,300 feet higher than Nazareth.

Picture how hard this journey would be for Mary, who was extremely pregnant and about to give birth. Today, women are advised to take it easy during the last weeks of their pregnancy.

During this journey, Mary would have probably traveled by donkey. It was surely a difficult and bumpy ride along dirty, dusty roads.

From our human point of view, we would think that this would be a terrible time to have a child. Yet seen from God's perspective, this was the fulfillment of a prophecy. The Messiah, the Savior of the world, was prophesied to be born in Bethlehem, and God used a Roman census to accomplish His purposes.

Think of Mary and Joseph's thoughts as they traveled. They were relatively poor, and so they probably did not have a great deal of money for the trip. Others may have traveled with them, but they were leaving their home behind.

Where did they stay each night? Did Mary go to sleep each night not knowing whether the baby would be born the next day? Did she and Joseph have doubts and concerns?

CHAPTER 22

No Room At The Inn

Mary and Joseph finally arrived at Bethlehem. An enormous event in human history was about to occur — the Son of God was about to come to earth, and be born of a woman. One would think that all of Bethlehem and all of Israel would rejoice, that the celebration would be the equivalent of fireworks filling the sky, and everyone would come to worship the newborn baby.

However, in truth, when the Savior was about to be born, there was no room for them at the inn. A small town such as Bethlehem in those days would probably have one major inn, which would be much like today's hotels — a resting place for weary travelers. No doubt because of the census, Bethlehem was full, and the rooms in the inn — which was probably quite small to begin with — were all taken.

One would think that even if the rooms were taken, someone would have given their room up to Joseph and Mary, who was obviously pregnant.

Even though it was prophesied that the Savior would be born in Bethlehem, Jesus could have been born in the comfort of an inn. What would you and I have done if we were there in Bethlehem — and what would we do today? Will we make room in our lives for Jesus? Will we let Him take first place in our lives — even if it means moving out of our comfort zone?

If the Son of God came calling for you today — would you receive Him?

CHAPTER 23

Jesus Is Born!

Joseph and Mary finally arrived in Bethlehem — the awaited time had come. The prophecy was being fulfilled — the Savior was ready to be born.

Finally, there in the little town of Bethlehem, Mary gave birth to her firstborn Son. Jesus the Savior was born! It was the first Christmas day. For centuries since that time, people all over the world have celebrated the birth of Jesus Christ, the Savior of the world.

What the angel told Mary and Joseph had come true — the Son of God had come to earth in the form of a baby. Mary the virgin had conceived and born a son whose name would be Jesus, and He would save His people from their sins.

When baby Jesus was born, Mary wrapped Him in cloths and placed him in a manger. While this sounds very picturesque, and we have all seen many beautiful manger scenes, a manger is actually a feeding trough for animals.

Mary and Joseph would have probably placed

fresh straw into the feeding trough, wrapped baby Jesus in cloths, and laid Him there in His make-shift crib. Truly the song "Away in a manger, no crib for a bed, the little Lord Jesus laid down His sweet head" is very appropriate.

Think of the range of emotions that Mary and Joseph must have felt there in the stable. In some ways, they may have felt peaceful and protected. Perhaps cows, donkeys, and other barnyard animals joined them there that night.

At the same time, it would not have been the cleanest place to lay a newborn baby. Instead of today's clean and sterile hospital rooms, the newborn baby was now in a place used by barnyard animals as bedroom, bathroom, and kitchen.

Did Mary and Joseph worry about the cleanliness and hygiene? If it had been you or me, we certainly would have worried. However, right from the beginning, God was displaying His power in the midst of weakness, and proving His ability to protect the baby Jesus from harm even in the middle of a stable.

CHAPTER 24

Mary And Joseph

Picture how Mary and Joseph must have felt. It was a joyous time — the Savior, the King of the world, had been born! The child they had waited for had come safely to this earth, and their hearts must have been filled with great joy.

At the same time, we must also remember that they were away from family. They had no place to stay and were forced to take shelter in a stable — a place for animals. Because of the census, Bethlehem was quite busy, and there was no room for the young family at the inn. The birth of a child is a personal, private time — and yet they did not even have a room to stay in.

We can only imagine how Joseph must have felt as a husband. A husband, during that time, was viewed as the provider and protector of his family. Joseph must have felt very vulnerable, and perhaps like he was not doing his job well.

How must Mary have felt? It had been prophesied to her that she would bear the Son of God, and she knew it was true, since she was, indeed, a virgin. Yet here she was in the town of Bethlehem, days away from home, without even a room of her own where she could give birth to her child in private.

Think of the mix of emotions that Mary and Joseph must have felt — joy at the birth of Jesus the Savior, relief that Jesus had been born safely, and praise to God for what He had done. Yet all this happened in a stable, since there was no room for them in the inn.

CHAPTER 25

The King Comes To Earth

Think for a minute about how the King of Kings came to this earth. One would think He would come to the capital city of Jerusalem, but instead, He came to the little town of Bethlehem.

We would think He would deserve a huge amount of attention and fanfare, but instead, He was ignored by almost everyone. As a king, He deserved to be born in a palace, but instead, even as the greatest king to ever be born, He was born and placed in a stable, a feeding place for animals.

If a king were to be born today, or almost any other time in history, he would get the best of care. In the stable, there may have been no one besides Mary and Joseph to watch over and protect the baby Jesus.

As a king, He deserved a crib of the finest silk, but instead, our king was placed in a manger, a feeding trough for animals.

While our hearts go out to the baby Jesus and to Mary and Joseph in this situation, we must also remember that God can do anything. God chose to make His appearance among mankind not in pride, but in humility; not in power, but in lowliness.

CHAPTER 26

Good News Of Great Joy

Even though most of Bethlehem was unaware that a King had been born in their midst, the word was about to spread to the most unlikely people — the shepherds living in the fields nearby, who kept watch over their flocks at night. "An angel of the Lord appeared to them, and the glory of the Lord shone around them, and they were terrified."[1]

Suddenly, an angel appears to shepherds out in the fields. Shepherds at that time were not people of particularly high social standing; they cared for sheep, who were an essential part of the area's economy, but also tended to be fairly dirty animals. And yet here, to lowly shepherds, an angel appeared to give them the glorious news. Why to shepherds? Perhaps it is God once again making the point that the good news of Christ is for all people, beginning with those who are poor and lowly. Then again, perhaps the shepherds had hearts that would listen. Perhaps the people in the busy town of Bethlehem were too occupied to make room for Mary and Joseph at the inn, and they may not even have heard an angel.

The shepherds were terrified; who among them had ever seen an angel before? We can only imagine that the appearance of an angel must have been absolutely awe inspiring to the shepherds.

The angel spoke to them and said, "Do not be afraid. I bring you good news of great joy that will be for all the people."[2]

Once again, the first thing the angel said to the shepherds is "do not be afraid."[3] Interestingly, these are the exact same words that the angel spoke to Zechariah and then to Mary, which gives us an idea of how amazing an experience it must have been to actually have seen an angel.

The angel announces "good news of great joy that will be for <u>all</u> the people."[4] Even though this message was just being given to the shepherds, the news they were about to hear would be for all people. Truly Jesus is the Savior who came to all mankind — to as many as would receive Him. "To all who received Him, to those who believed in His name, He gave the right to become children of God…"[5]

Even though they were just shepherds, they were about to receive good news of great joy which would be for all people for all time.

CHAPTER 27

Christ The Lord

The angel continued, "Today in the town of David a Savior has been born to you; He is Christ the Lord."[1]

Here is the most wonderful news that has ever been heard — Christ had been born that very day, right there in Bethlehem, which is the town of David.

And this was not just any birth — it was the birth of a Savior, who is Christ the Lord. Think about each of these words.

First, He is a Savior. As had been prophesied, Jesus came to save people from their sins; to reconcile mankind, with all of our sins and wrongs, to a holy God. This was the most wonderful news in the world. The very name Jesus means "God is salvation;" truly, God is our Savior.

It is then, for the first time, that Jesus is called "Christ." Today, we use the term "Jesus Christ" as if it was Jesus' first and last name, but that is not the case.

The baby's given name was Jesus. Christ is

and was the title of the Messiah; the Savior of the world. This was the Savior whose coming had been prophesied and who the Jews had been waiting for to save their people.

Christ means "the Anointed One." The priests of old were anointed with oil — oil was placed on their forehead — as a symbol of God's favor. The Anointed One was God's chosen one to deliver His people. Christ was not a political or military ruler, who would deliver His people from Roman occupation; He was the Savior of the world, who would offer the ability to be saved from sin to all who would believe. Governments like Rome may come and go, but sin remains. Christ can deliver us from sin.

The angel also called Jesus "the Lord," a title of great authority. Christ is not just any Lord, He is the Lord of all mankind. The shepherds were perhaps the first to hear — in Bethlehem had been born the Savior of the world who is Christ, the Chosen One and Lord of all.

CHAPTER 28

Glory To God

The angel then announced to the shepherds, "This will be a sign to you; you will find a baby wrapped in cloths and lying in a manger."[1]

How great is the majesty of God! First the angels gave the news of a Savior for all mankind, who is Christ, the Chosen One, the Lord. Surely the shepherds could be forgiven if they expected this baby to be in a king's palace, or at the very least in the finest residence in Bethlehem. Perhaps they would have expected an army of soldiers and an armed guard of Romans.

Instead, the sign they were given is that the baby would be wrapped in cloths and would lie in a manger.

Think of this! Here is the announcement of the birth of Jesus, who is a king — and not just any king, but a king who is God's son — and yet He is born in poverty and lying in a manger. God displays His power in weakness.

"Suddenly a great company of the heavenly host appeared with the angel, praising God and saying, 'Glory to God in the highest, and on earth peace to men on whom His favor rests.'"[2] Now there is not just one angel, but a great number of angels filling the night. Did the angels appear only to the shepherds? Is it possible that there were angels singing in Bethlehem and all over the world, but no one stopped to listen?

We don't really know, but we do know that the shepherds saw and heard a great multitude of these angels giving praise to God.

The message they sang was "Glory to God in the highest," a beautiful song which has been passed down to generations as "Gloria in excelsis Deo" which is the Latin translation of "Glory to God in the highest." The angels gave glory to God at the birth of Christ the Lord.

The angels also announced peace to mankind. However, this was not peace of an earthly sort, because unfortunately wars have continued to this day. This is peace with God for those who receive Christ as Lord and Savior. We could now have peace in our hearts because peace between man and God is now freely available through Jesus Christ our Lord.

CHAPTER 29

Peace With God

How can you have peace in your heart with God? It is by welcoming Christ into your life. Don't be like the people in the inn who were too busy for Jesus. Rather, be like the shepherds who listened to the word about Christ and then ran to see Jesus.

The name Jesus means "God is Salvation." Jesus came to this earth to be your salvation. Will you welcome Him in?

If you want to receive Christ as your Savior and Lord, you can pray this prayer. "Lord Jesus, I welcome You into my heart and life as my Savior and Lord. Thank You for dying on the cross and forgiving my sins. You alone can bring salvation to me. Please live in my life always. Amen."

If you have sincerely prayed this prayer, you have asked Christ into your life. I encourage you to go tell someone you know that you have received Christ as your Savior.

CHAPTER 30

The Shepherds Respond

The shepherds responded in obedience to what the angel had told them. "When the angels had left them and gone into heaven, the shepherds said to one another, 'Let's go to Bethlehem and see this thing that has happened, which the Lord has told us about.'

"So they hurried off and found Mary and Joseph, and the baby, who was lying in the manger. When they had seen Him, they spread the word concerning what had been told about this child, and all who heard it were amazed at what the shepherds said to them. But Mary treasured up all these things and pondered them in her heart. The shepherds returned, glorifying and praising God for all the things they had heard and seen, which were just as they had been told."[1]

The shepherds believed what they had heard and went to see Jesus. Just as had been told them, they came and found Mary, Joseph, and baby Jesus, who was lying in the manger. How Mary and Joseph must have been amazed when the shepherds came in, as they must have told them what the angel had said — that in the city of Bethlehem had been born a Savior who is Christ the Lord!

And the shepherds did not stop there; once they had seen Jesus, they spread the word to others about what they had heard about Christ. As far as we know, these shepherds were the first human witnesses to tell others about Jesus. They then returned to their fields, praising God for everything being just as the angel had told them.

CHAPTER 31

His Name Is Jesus

Just as had happened with John the Baptist, eight days after Jesus was born the time came for Him to be circumcised. At the time of circumcision, a Jewish baby's name was officially given. Here the baby was given the name of Jesus — God is salvation. Both Mary and Joseph had been given this name by the angel who had appeared to them separately. And so for all time the child would be known as Jesus.

When Jesus was about six weeks old, He made His first trip to Jerusalem. "Joseph and Mary took Him to Jerusalem to present Him to the Lord,"[1] in accordance with Jewish custom which said "Every first born male is to be consecrated to the Lord."[2]

There, Mary and Joseph offered a sacrifice in accordance with Jewish law. Depending on the financial resources of the family, those who were more well to do would offer a lamb to sacrifice; those who were poor would offer a pair of doves or two young pigeons. Since Mary and Joseph did not have much money, they offered the smaller sacrifice. Here was Christ, the Lord of the entire universe, whom God had chosen in His humility to come and be born to parents of modest means, who could only afford the smaller of two sacrifices. God is wonderful in His humility.

This was Jesus' first trip to Jerusalem after being born. His last trip to Jerusalem during His time on earth was to be about 33 years later, when He came to Jerusalem to be crucified. This last trip would be to die on a cross to pay for the sins of the world; but on this, His first trip, He came to the temple, which was built to worship God. It was very appropriate and symbolic for Jesus to be there. He came as a little baby, with all the limitations of a baby; yet, in the midst of the temple, for anyone who would recognize Him, here was God in the flesh.

CHAPTER 32

Simeon

Living in Jerusalem at this time was a man called Simeon. He was a righteous and godly man who was waiting to see the Messiah, the Savior.

"It had been revealed to him by the Holy Spirit that he would not die before he had seen the Lord's Christ. Moved by the Spirit, he went into the temple courts. When the parents brought in the child Jesus to do for Him what the custom of the law required, Simeon took Him in his arms and praised God, saying: 'Sovereign Lord, as You have promised, You now dismiss Your servant in peace. For my eyes have seen Your salvation, which You have prepared in the sight of all people, a light for revelation to the Gentiles and for glory to your people Israel.'"[1]

We once again see a continuing theme. Simeon talks about Jesus as salvation — and not only salvation for the Jewish people but a light of revelation for the Gentiles, which is the term referring to all those who are not Jewish. Jesus was to offer salvation to the whole world.

Mary and Joseph marveled at what Simeon said about Christ. "Then Simeon blessed them and said to Mary, His mother: 'This child is destined to cause the falling and rising of many in Israel, and to be a sign that will be spoken against, so that the thoughts of many hearts will be revealed. And a sword will pierce your own soul too.'"[2]

Along with his encouraging words, Simeon brought a warning — that a sword would pierce Mary's own soul. As we know, Mary's own soul would indeed experience great pain years later when she would behold her son Jesus dying on a cross to pay the penalty for the sins of the world.

CHAPTER 33

Anna

Another stranger approached Mary, Joseph, and the baby Jesus while they were in the temple. Her name was Anna, and she was a prophetess, a godly woman who spoke prophecies as God inspired her.

"She was very old; she had lived with her husband seven years after her marriage, and then was a widow until she was eighty-four. She never left the temple but worshiped night and day, fasting and praying."[1]

She came up to Joseph, Mary, and Jesus at that very moment. "She gave thanks to God and spoke about the child to all who were looking forward to the redemption of Jerusalem."[2]

Once again, someone whose heart was seeking God recognized Jesus even though He was just a tiny baby. The temple in Jerusalem was a busy place, and quite possibly on that day there could have been hundreds of people in the temple. Also, it was the custom of the Jewish people for all first born males to be presented to the Lord,

and so there may have been many Jewish babies presented that day. Why would Anna and Simeon recognize Jesus as the Christ, when His parents were poor and only able to afford the smallest offering? It was because their hearts were sensitive to God and they recognized Christ for who He truly was. Anna and Simeon saw with spiritual eyes, not just physical eyes.

CHAPTER 34

The Magi

"After Jesus was born in Bethlehem in Judea, during the time of King Herod, Magi from the east came to Jerusalem and asked, 'Where is the one who has been born king of the Jews? We saw His star in the east and have come to worship Him.'"[1]

Magi were possibly members of a ruling caste who came from lands located to the east of Israel — perhaps Persia or modern day Saudi Arabia. The Magi were men who were exceedingly wise, and who studied the stars, history, and perhaps even the religions of other lands. While we have no exact equivalent for "Magi" in today's world, they have been called "wise men" and "kings" over the centuries.

These Magi became the first people who were not Jewish to worship Jesus. Until now, the people we have seen — the shepherds, Mary, Joseph, Elizabeth — are all Jewish. Now, people from other nations of the world begin to seek out Christ — a process that continues to this very day.

CHAPTER 35

The Star

The Magi talked about seeing "His star" in the east, and they recognized this star as announcing the birth of the one who was born king of the Jews.

We don't know exactly what star it was that they saw, but we do know that they were not just seeing the regular stars in the heavens, because after the wise men left Jerusalem they followed the star to Bethlehem until it shone above where Jesus lay. God had provided a miracle of a star so powerful that it drew the wise men to come and see Jesus.

They must have traveled a long journey, for "lands of the east" probably meant lands hundreds of miles away, and travel was slow in those days. God honored the wise men's search for Him, even from a great distance.

Did other people see the star? Perhaps they did, but just ignored it and went about their busy lives. It's just like in Bethlehem — Mary and Joseph came right to the inn, but people were too busy and selfish to receive them and give room for the baby Jesus. But the wise men, who were looking for God, found Him when He appeared.

CHAPTER 36

King Of Israel

The Magi came to Jerusalem asking a startling question, "Where is the one who has been born king of the Jews?"[1] Imagine the uproar and consternation this must have caused, particularly in the household of King Herod, for King Herod thought that he was the only king of the Jews.

King Herod was a "puppet ruler," in that he ruled Israel, but only because he was allowed to do so by the Roman powers. He was a cruel and vicious man. History records that Herod murdered his own wife and three sons. He was jealous of power, and now suddenly Magi from the east have appeared asking who has been born king of the Jews. Little did Herod know that while he may have been the temporary king of the Jews in an earthly sense, Jesus who had been born would be king of the Jews and of all nations for all time.

"When King Herod heard this, he was disturbed and all Jerusalem with him. When he had called together all the people's chief priests and teachers of the law, he asked them where the Christ was to be born."[2]

CHAPTER 37

The King Is In Bethlehem

When Herod asked the chief priests and teachers of the law where the Christ was to be born, they answered, "In Bethlehem in Judea, for this is what the prophet has written..."[1] They then quoted the Prophet Micah, who seven centuries before had said "But you, Bethlehem, in the land of Judah, are by no means least among the rulers of Judah; for out of you will come a ruler who will be the shepherd of my people Israel."[2] The chief priests and teachers of the law knew the scriptures and correctly identified Bethlehem as the place where the Christ, Savior and King of the Jews, was to be born.

"Then Herod called the Magi secretly and found out from them the exact time the star had appeared. He sent them to Bethlehem and said, 'Go and make a careful search for the child. As soon as you find him, report to me, so that I too may go and worship him.'"[3] It is here that we see the evil that can lurk in a man's heart. Did King Herod really intend to go and worship Jesus? No, he did not. Consumed by jealousy, Herod wanted no one but himself to be king. The wise men, however, truly had hearts to worship Jesus, and so they set off to Bethlehem to find Jesus.

CHAPTER 38

The Magi Find Jesus

After the Magi had met with King Herod, "They went on their way, and the star they had seen in the east went ahead of them until it stopped over the place where the child was. When they saw the star, they were overjoyed. On coming to the house, they saw the child with His mother Mary, and they bowed down and worshiped Him. Then they opened their treasures and presented Him with gifts of gold and of incense and of myrrh."[1]

God led the Magi by the star, right to the place where Jesus was. Just as the shepherds came to worship Jesus, now the non-Jewish Magi from the east bowed down and gave worship to the baby.

Picture this sight. The Magi from the east are probably either kings, or at least wise men with great wealth. They have already met in Jerusalem with King Herod, in all his power and glory. Now, they have come to the small, humble town of Bethlehem and find the baby Jesus with Mary and Joseph. And yet, even after having seen King Herod in all his glory and now seeing the baby Jesus in His humble circumstances, the Magi have the wisdom and the heart for God to bow down and worship Christ. They know in their hearts that this is God, and they fall down to worship Him.

The Magi presented their magnificent and symbolic gifts. Gold was the money of the day, and was symbolic of kings. Incense was used in the temple for the worship of God. Myrrh was a spice which was of great value and was used, among other things, to anoint bodies for burial.

Even in their gifts, the Magi worshiped Christ as King; they worshiped Him as God; and unknowingly, they foretold His death. For truly, Jesus is King, He is God, and He was to die for the sins of the world.

When the Magi had worshiped Christ, they were warned in a dream not to go back to King Herod, and so they returned to their country by another route.

CHAPTER 39

What Happens Next

What happened next? Well, that's a long story. Following are some of the key events.

Joseph was warned in a dream to escape from King Herod, who would try to kill Jesus. Joseph and Mary took the baby Jesus and they fled to Egypt until Herod was dead. When Herod died, they returned to Israel and to Nazareth where they had originally lived. Jesus grew up as a young man in the town of Nazareth.

When He was about thirty years old, Jesus began His public ministry. Interestingly enough, His public ministry began when He was baptized at the river Jordan by John the Baptist — who was once the baby that rejoiced in the womb when Jesus came to him. As a young man, John the Baptist had a ministry where he proclaimed the way of the Lord and prepared people for the Savior who was to come.

For the next three years, Jesus taught people about God. He healed the sick; He raised the dead, and He performed many miracles. Thousands of people listened to His teachings, and Jesus poured His life into them and into His twelve disciples who followed Him closely. He displayed the love of God to the multitudes, He ministered to the poor, and He cared for the weak and outcast.

CHAPTER 40

His Time Has Come

After about three years of public ministry, the time had come for Jesus to give His life for the sins of the world. Even though Jesus had lived His life perfectly and sinlessly as had been prophesied, He willingly went to Jerusalem where He was arrested and tried.

The charge against Him was that He claimed to be the Messiah, the Son of God. He was found guilty and sentenced to death by execution. He was condemned to be nailed to a wooden cross. Even though Jesus had the power of God at His disposal and could have called down legions of angels to stop the execution, He willingly went to the cross to take the punishment that you and I deserve. All of us like sheep have gone astray from God, and have sinned and done or thought things that are wrong. Jesus, though He was sinless, took our punishment in our place. As had been prophesied, and as His name says, "God is Salvation." Jesus is the Savior of the world.

Jesus died on the cross, and His disciples

despaired. However, three days later He rose from the dead, and He appeared alive to hundreds of people over the next several weeks. He then rose miraculously into heaven, where He lives today at the right hand of God, His Father. Someday, Jesus Christ will come to earth again where He will reign forever as King of Kings and Lord of Lords.

CHAPTER 41

You And Me

The most important question in the world for you and me today is: How will we welcome Jesus? Will we…

Ignore Him, like the crowds in Bethlehem? They had Christ right in their midst and yet were too busy to let Him into their lives. Or will we…

Reject Him, like Herod who wanted no king but himself on the throne? Or will we…

Welcome Him into our lives? Will you welcome Christ as Savior and Lord — like Mary, Joseph, Elizabeth, and the shepherds? Like Simeon, Anna, and the three wise men, you too can come and worship Christ. All of these people acted on faith. They did not have the "whole picture" as we do today, yet they still believed that Jesus Christ was the Savior of the world and they welcomed Him as their Lord and Savior.

CHAPTER 42

You Can Welcome Christ Today

It's not too late to welcome Jesus Christ into your heart and life today. "Yet to all who received Him, to those who believed in His name, He gave the right to become children of God…" [1]

How can we receive Christ? We can receive Christ in much the same way as Elizabeth, the wise men and the shepherds — by believing that Jesus Christ is your Savior and that He is God.

If you would like to welcome Jesus Christ into your life as your Savior and Lord, by believing that He died on the cross for your sins, you can ask Him into your life by praying a prayer like this: "Lord Jesus, I need You. Thank You for dying on the cross for my sins. I receive You as my Savior and my Lord. Thank You for coming to earth to give me the gift of eternal life and salvation."

If you have welcomed Christ into your life, I encourage you to contact a Christian friend or your local church so that they can help you learn how to follow Christ as Savior and Lord all the days of your life.

May God Bless you this Christmas.

www.TheNativity.com

Scripture References

13. Zechariah's Prophecy
[1] Luke 1:68 – 71
[2] Luke 1:72 – 75
[3] Luke 1:76 – 77
[4] Luke 1:78 – 79

15. Joseph's Dream
[1] Matthew 1:20
[2] Matthew 1:20, 21

17. Isaiah's Prophecy
[1] Matthew 1:23
[2] Isaiah 9:6
[3] John 1:1, 14

19. Joseph Responds
[1] Matthew 1:24

26. Good News of Great Joy
[1] Luke 2:9
[2] Luke 2:10
[3] Luke 2:10
[4] Luke 2:10
[5] John 1:12

27. Christ the Lord
[1] Luke 2:11

28. Glory to God
[1] Luke 2:12
[2] Luke 2:13, 14

30. The Shepherds Respond
[1] Luke 2:15 – 20

31. His Name is Jesus
[1] Luke 2:22
[2] Luke 2:23

32. Simeon
[1] Luke 2:26 – 32
[2] Luke 2:34, 35

33. Anna
[1] Luke 2:36, 37
[2] Luke 2:38

34. The Magi
[1] Matthew 2:1, 2

36. King of Israel
[1] Matthew 2:2
[2] Matthew 2:3, 4

37. The King is in Bethlehem
[1] Matthew 2:5
[2] Matthew 2:6
[3] Matthew 2:7, 8

38. The Magi Find Jesus
[1] Matthew 2:9 - 11

42. You Can Welcome Christ Today
[1] John 1:12